Cambridge Young Learners English Tests

Cambridge Starters 6

Examination papers from

University of Cambridge
ESOL Examinations:

English for Speakers of Other Languages

CAMBRIDGE UNIVERSITY PRESS
Cambridge, New York, Melbourne, Madrid, Cape Town,
Singapore, São Paulo, Delhi, Mexico City

Cambridge University Press
The Edinburgh Building, Cambridge CB2 8RU, UK

www.cambridge.org
Information on this title: www.cambridge.org/9780521739337

© Cambridge University Press 2009

This publication is in copyright. Subject to statutory exception
and to the provisions of relevant collective licensing agreements,
no reproduction of any part may take place without the written
permission of Cambridge University Press.

First published 2009
7th printing 2013

Printed in Dubai by Oriental Press

A catalogue record for this publication is available from the British Library

ISBN 978-0-521-73933-7 Student's Book
ISBN 978-0-521-73934-4 Answer Booklet
ISBN 978-0-521-73935-1 Audio CD

Cover design by David Lawton
Produced by HL Studios

Cambridge University Press has no responsibility for the persistence or
accuracy of URLs for external or third-party internet websites referred to in
this publication, and does not guarantee that any content on such websites is,
or will remain, accurate or appropriate. Information regarding prices, travel
timetables and other factual information given in this work is correct at
the time of first printing but Cambridge University Press does not guarantee
the accuracy of such information thereafter.

Contents

Test 1
Listening — 5
Reading and Writing — 11

Test 2
Listening — 19
Reading and Writing — 25

Test 3
Listening — 33
Reading and Writing — 39

Speaking Tests
Test 1 — 47
Test 2 — 51
Test 3 — 55

Test 1
Listening

Part 1
– 5 questions –

Listen and draw lines. There is one example.

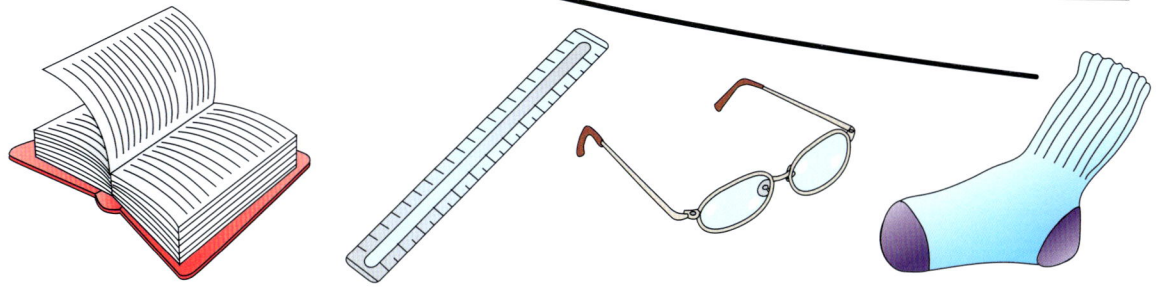

Part 2
– 5 questions –

Read the question. Listen and write a name or a number.

There are two examples.

Examples

What's the boy's name? ....Bill..................

How old is he? ....6..................

Questions

1   What's the name of Bill's toy monkey?   ....

2   How old is Bill's toy monkey?   ....

3   How many brothers and sisters
    has Bill got?   ....

4   What is Bill's mum's name?   ....

5   What's Bill's family name?   ....

Part 3
– 5 questions –

Listen and tick (✓) the box. There is one example.

What sport is on TV today?

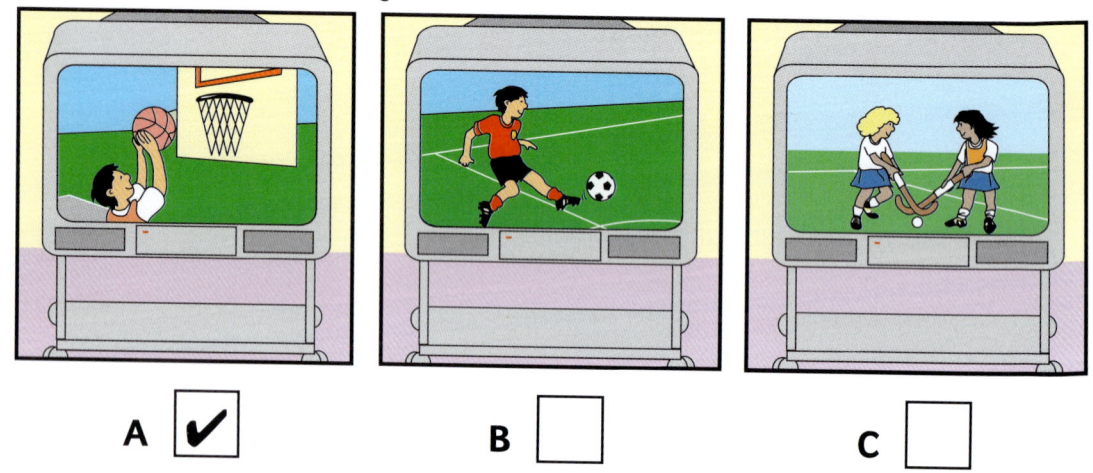

A ✓   B ☐   C ☐

1 Which is Sue's toy?

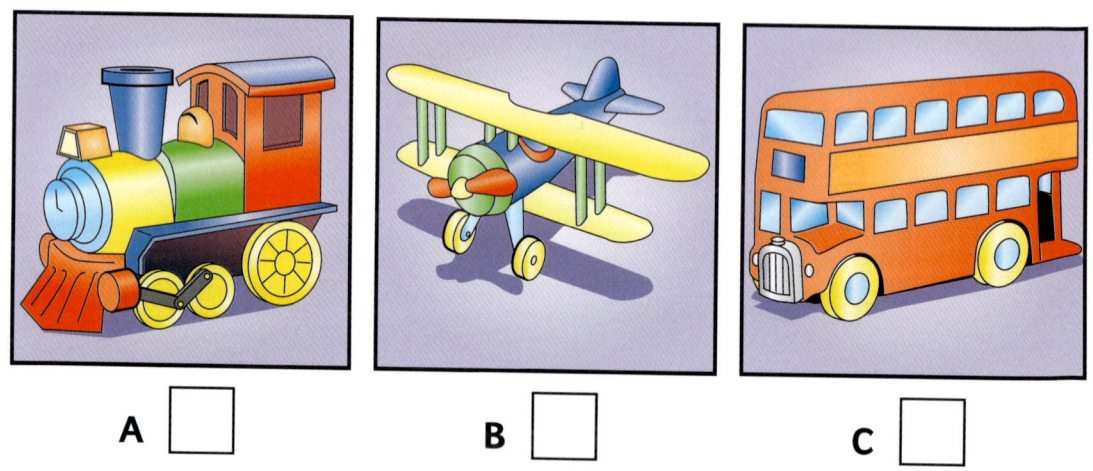

A ☐   B ☐   C ☐

2 Where are Tom's trousers?

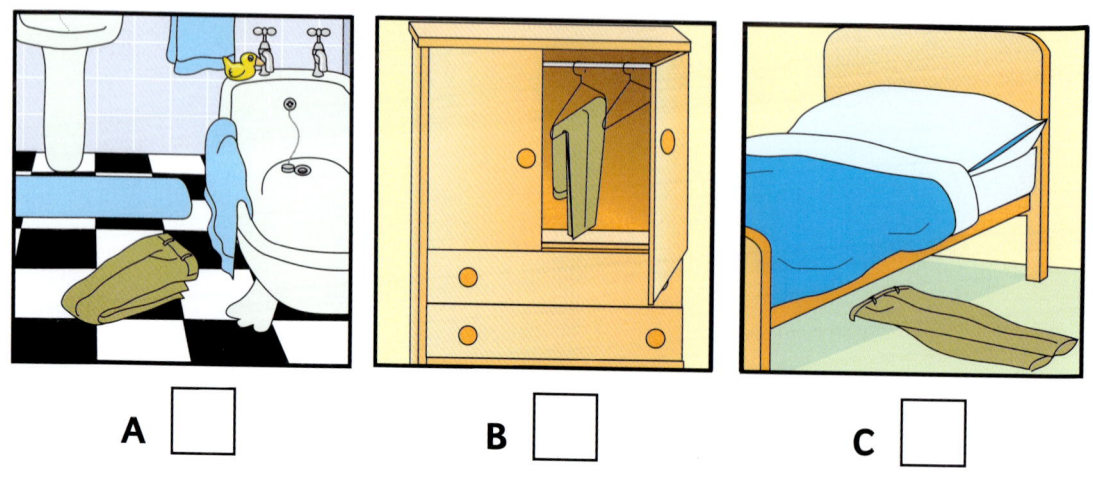

A ☐   B ☐   C ☐

3   Which book does Sam want?

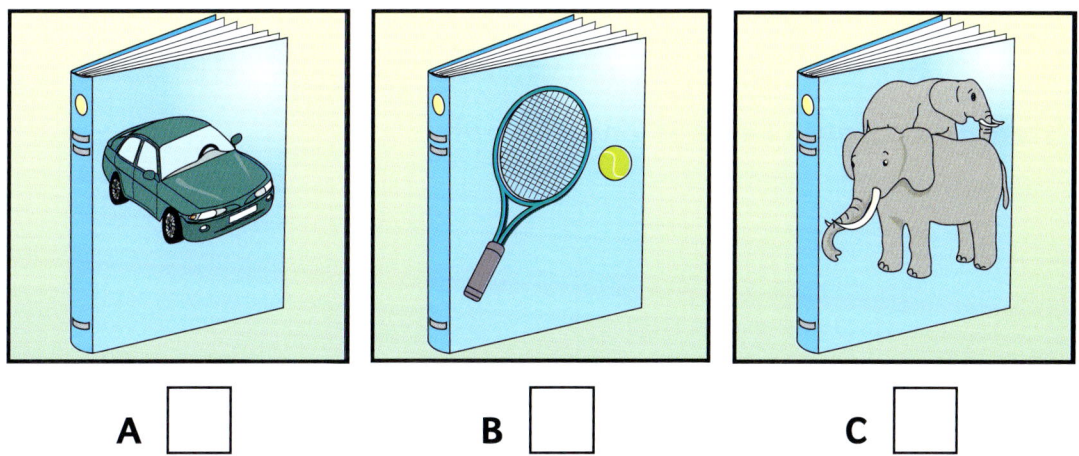

4   What is Ann drawing?

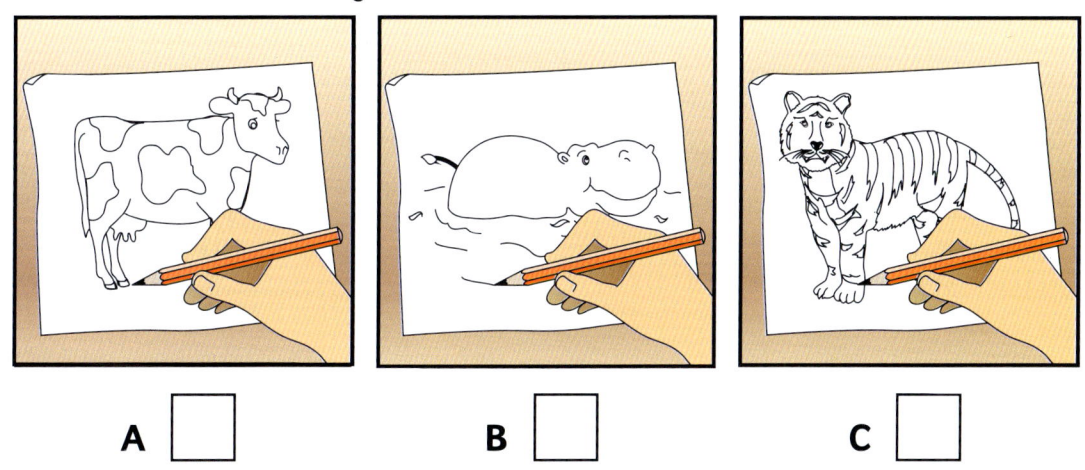

5   What can Ben's mum do?

Test 1

Part 4
– 5 questions –

Listen and colour. There is one example.

Test 1
Reading and Writing

Part 1
– 5 questions –

Look and read. Put a tick (✔) or a cross (✘) in the box.
There are two examples.

Examples

This is a car.

This is a goat.

Questions

1

This is a sofa.   ☐

Test 1

2  This is a lorry. ☐

3  This is a lizard.

4 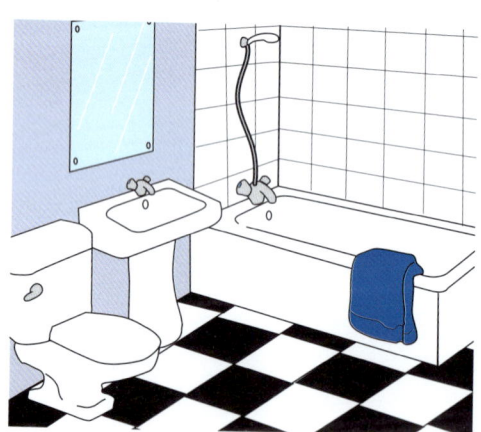 This is a bathroom.

5  This is a bird.

Part 2
– 5 questions –

Look and read. Write yes or no.

Examples

Two boys are playing basketball. ....yes.............

There is a cat in the garden. ....no.............

Questions

1   One of the children is wearing jeans. ....

2   A man is painting the window. ....

3   There is a kite in the tree. ....

4   Some chickens are drinking the water. ....

5   The dog has got short legs. ....

Test 1

Part 3
– 5 questions –

Look at the pictures. Look at the letters. Write the words.

Example

   <u>e</u> <u>g</u> <u>g</u>

Questions

1   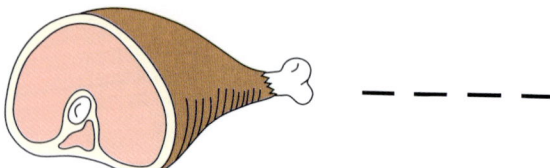   _ _ _ _

2   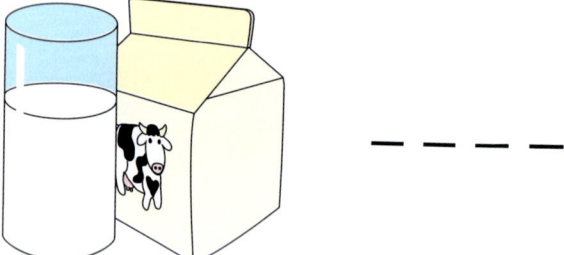   _ _ _ _

3      _ _ _ _ _

4   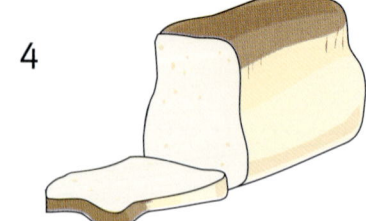   _ _ _ _ _

5   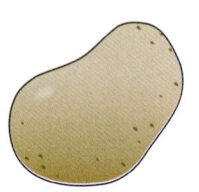   _ _ _ _ _ _

Part 4
– 5 questions –

Read this. Choose a word from the box. Write the correct word next to numbers 1–5. There is one example.

A computer

I am in a ....house....... or in a **(1)** .... I am

on a table or a desk. A person sits on a **(2)** .... in front

of me. All the **(3)** .... of the alphabet are on me.

(4) .... can learn with me and they like playing

(5) .... on me.

What am I? I am a computer.

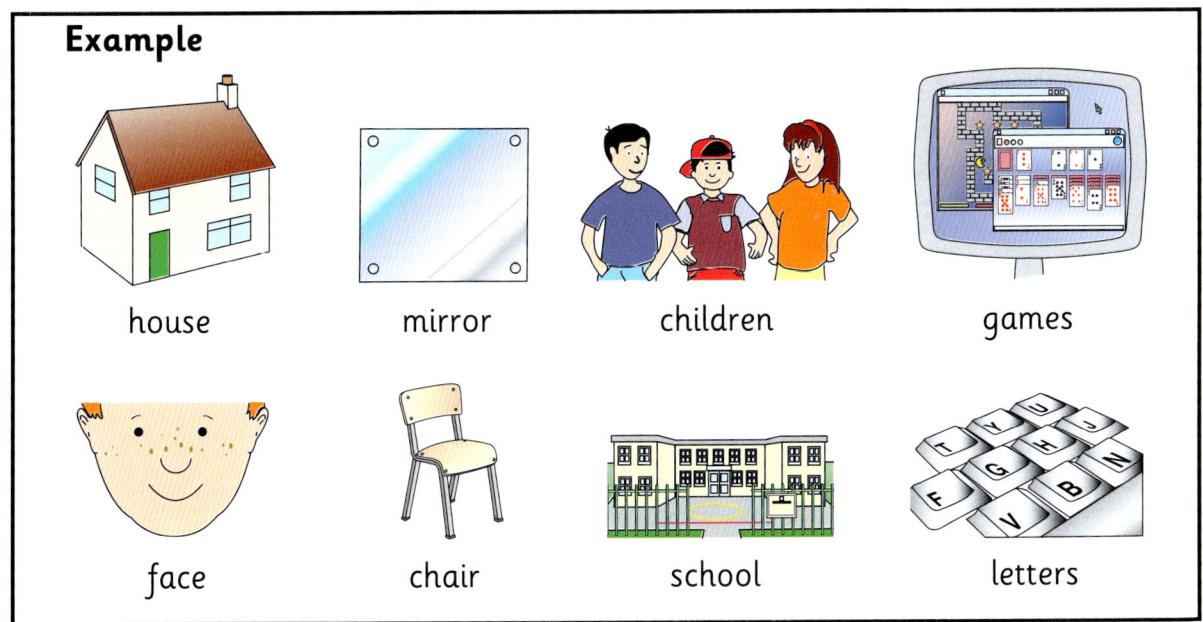

Part 5
– 5 questions –

Look at the pictures and read the questions. Write one-word answers.

Examples

Where is this?   on a .... train ....

How many bags are there?   .... two ....

Questions

1   What is the man doing?   ....

Reading and Writing

2   Who is the man talking to?   the ....

3   What has the girl got?   a ....

4   Where is the bag?   on the ....

5   What has the man got in his hands?   a ....

Blank Page

Test 2
Listening

Part 1
– 5 questions –

Listen and draw lines. There is one example.

19

Part 2
– 5 questions –

Read the question. Listen and write a name or a number.

There are two examples.

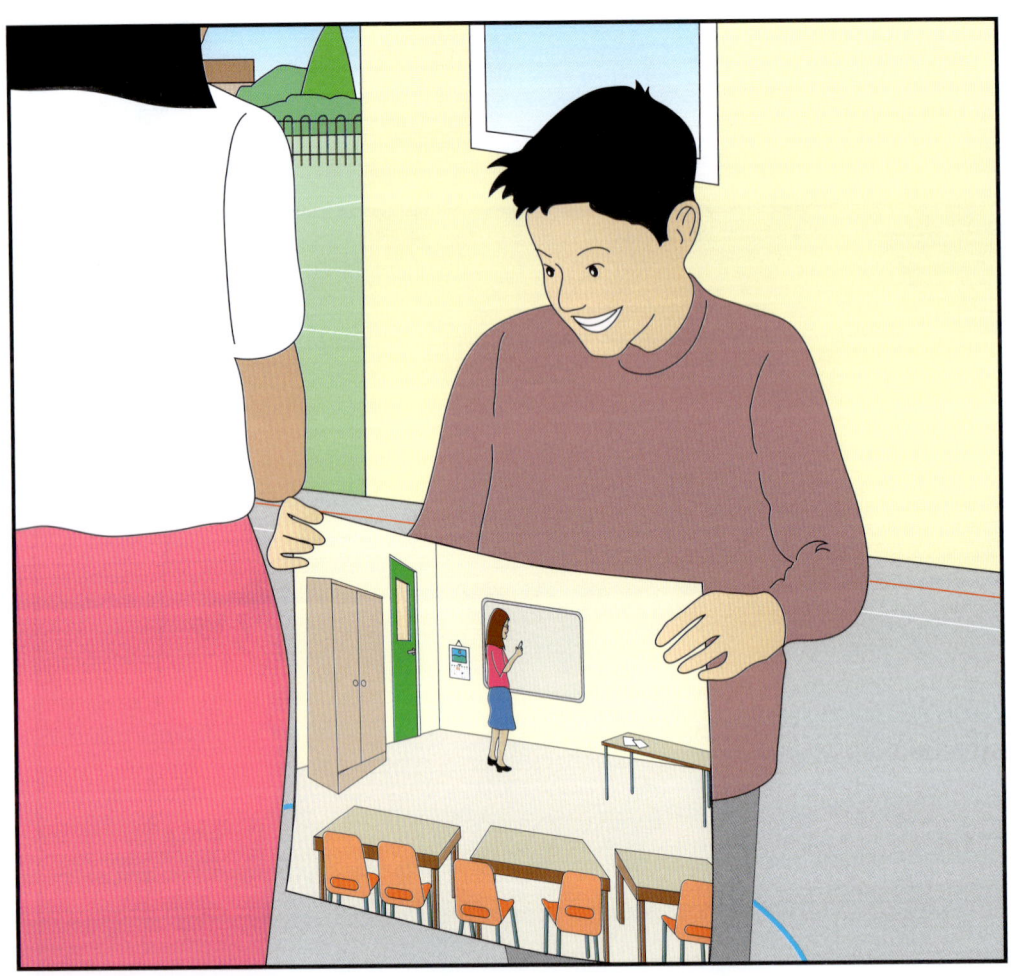

Examples

What's the boy's name? .... Pat ....

Which class is he in? .... 5 ....

Questions

1   What is Pat's friend's name?   ....

2   How many girls are in Pat's class?   ....

3   Who is the woman in Pat's picture?   Mrs
                                                    ....

4   How many mice has the woman got?   ....

5   Where does Pat live?   Street
                                                    ....

Part 3
– 5 questions –

Listen and tick (✔) the box. There is one example.

What's Mum doing?

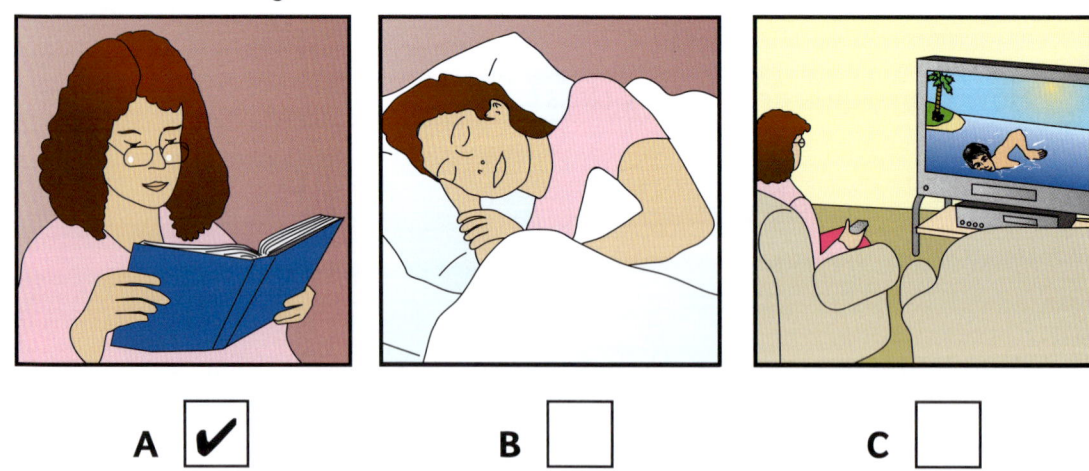

1 Where's the football shirt?

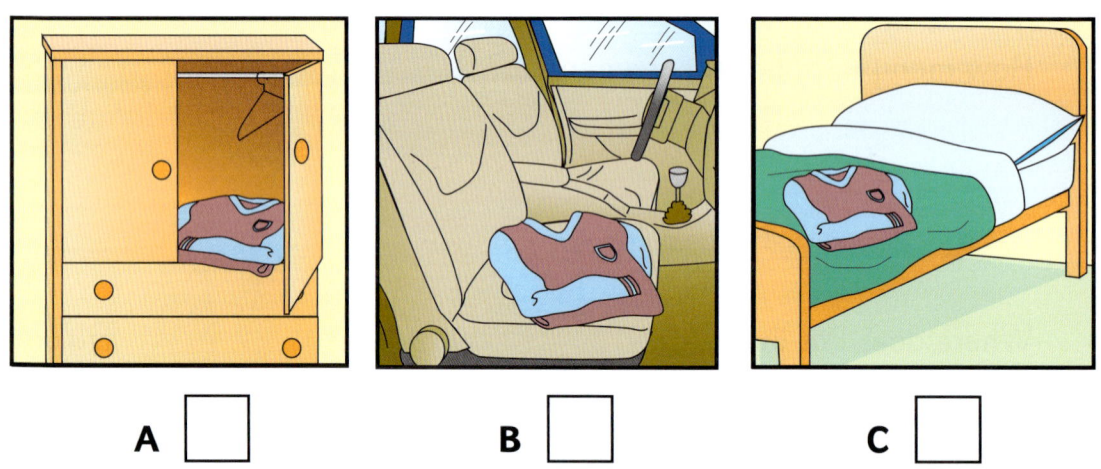

2 Which animals does Sue like?

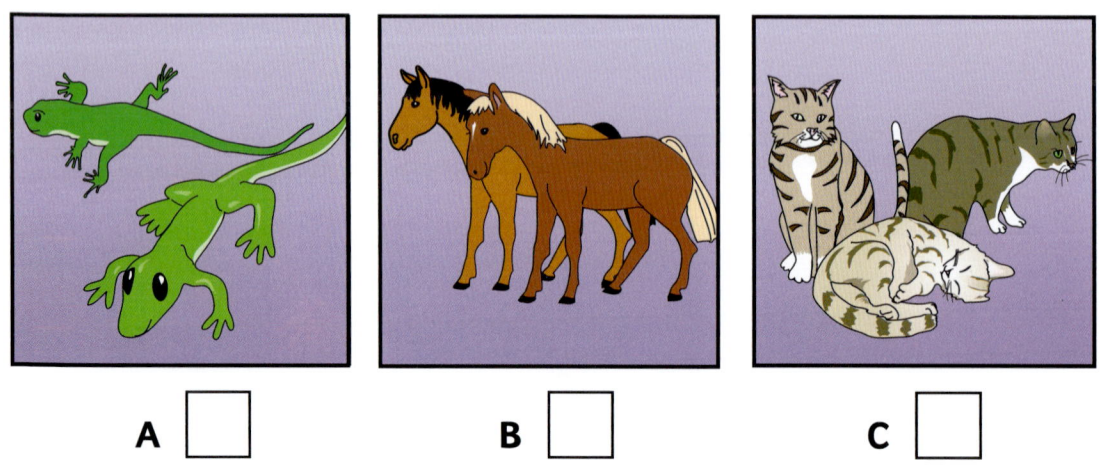

3 Where are Grandfather's glasses?

A ☐   B ☐   C ☐

4 Where can Mum put the spider?

A ☐   B ☐   C ☐

5 How old is Nick?

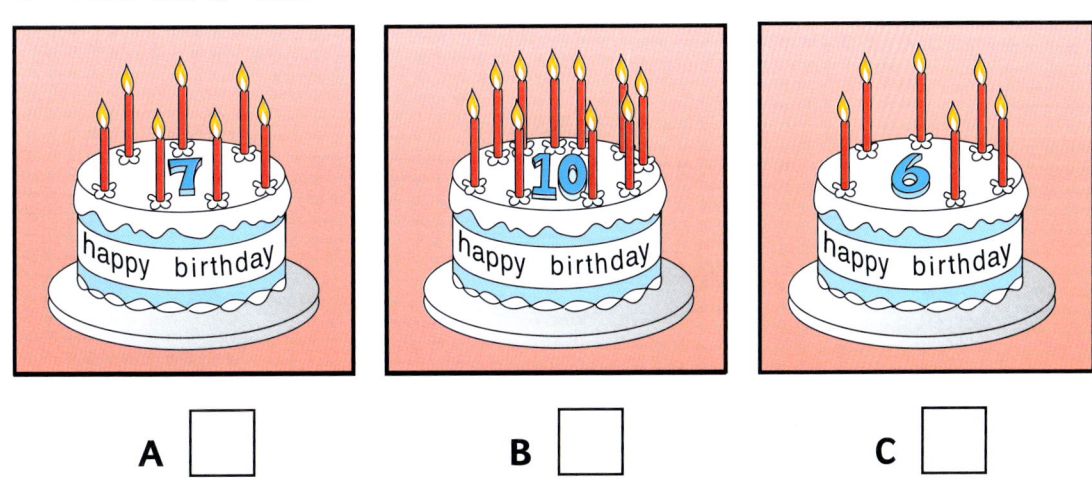

A ☐   B ☐   C ☐

Part 4
– 5 questions –

Listen and colour. There is one example.

Test 2
Reading and Writing

Part 1
– 5 questions –

Look and read. Put a tick (✔) or a cross (✗) in the box. There are two examples.

Examples

This is a sheep.

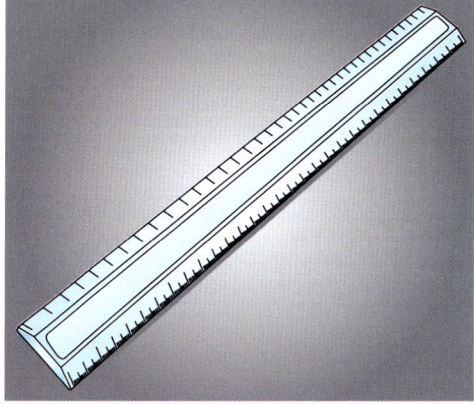

This is a rubber.

Questions

1

This is an onion.

Test 2

2  This is a plane. ☐

3  This is a giraffe.

4  This is a watermelon.

5  This is a letter.

Reading and Writing

Part 2
– 5 questions –

Look and read. Write yes or no.

Examples

The baby is sleeping.	yes
The toys are in the box.	no

Questions

1 The phone is on the floor. ....

2 The woman is sitting on the sofa. ....

3 There are some clothes in the garden. ....

4 A girl is playing the piano. ....

5 A mouse is running under the table. ....

Part 3
– 5 questions –

Look at the pictures. Look at the letters. Write the words.

Example

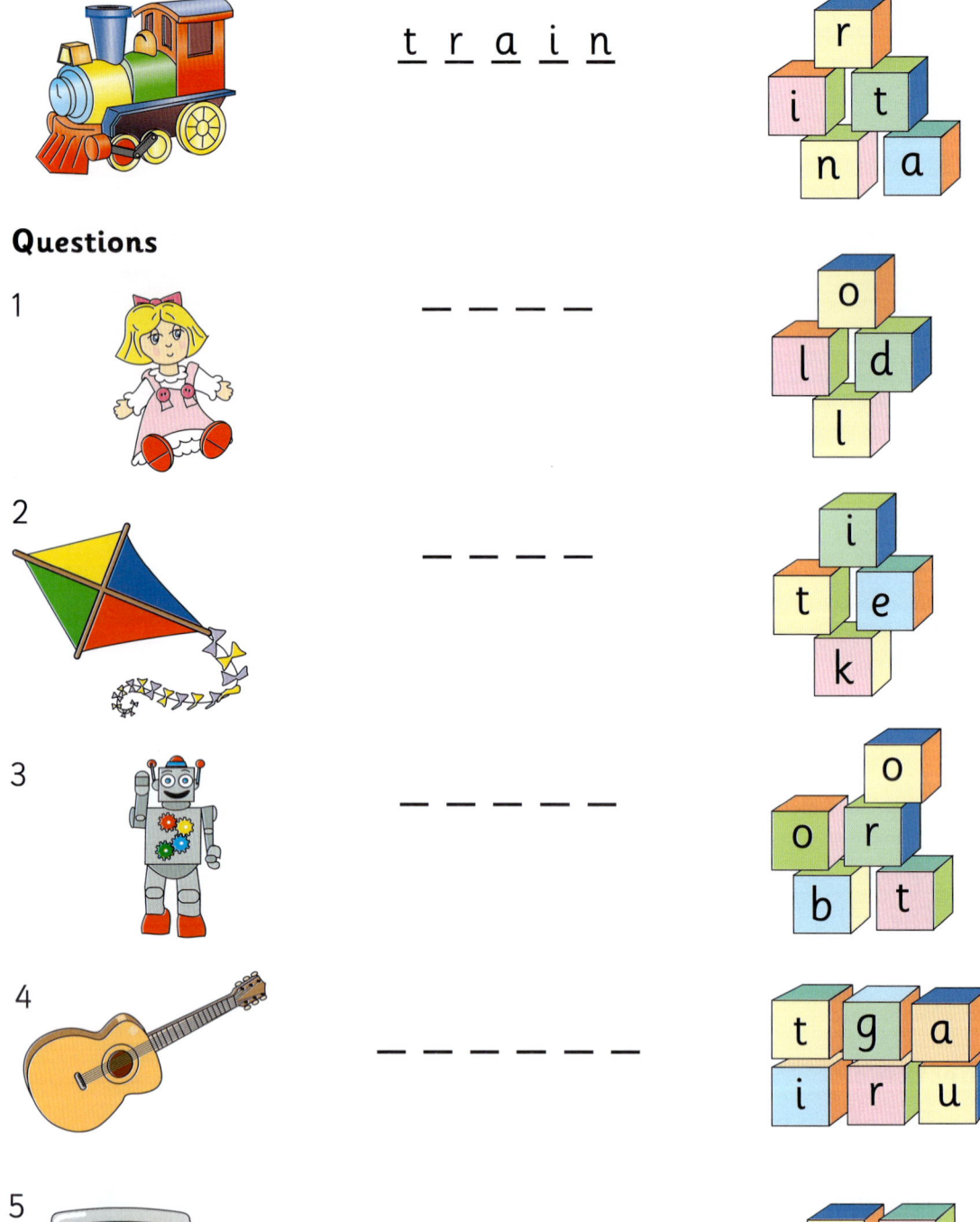

t r a i n

Questions

1 _ _ _ _

2 _ _ _ _

3 _ _ _ _ _

4 _ _ _ _ _ _

5 _ _ _ _ _ _ _ _

Part 4
– 5 questions –

Read this. Choose a word from the box. Write the correct word next to numbers 1–5. There is one example.

The sea

In ......*photos*.......... , I look blue, green or grey. People sit next to me on the beach. There are lots of beautiful **(1)** .... on the beach too. Big and small **(2)** .... swim in me under the water. People can go on me in a **(3)** .... Some children like walking next to me and they eat an ice cream or have a **(4)** .... They like swimming and playing with a **(5)** .... in me too.

What am I? I am the sea.

29

Test 2

Part 5
– 5 questions –

Look at the pictures and read the questions. Write one-word answers.

Examples

Who wants a drink?   the ......man......

How many crocodiles are there?   ......three......

Questions

1   Where is the monkey?   in the ....

Reading and Writing

2 What is the monkey throwing?   a ....

3 Where is the man's hand?   on his ....

4 What is the man doing now?   ....

5 What is the monkey wearing?   the ....

Blank Page

Test 3
Listening

Part 1
– 5 questions –

Listen and draw lines. There is one example.

Test 3

Part 2
– 5 questions –

Read the question. Listen and write a name or a number.

There are two examples.

Examples

Who can play the guitar?   May

How old is she?   8

Listening

Questions

1 Which class is May in? ....

2 What's the name of May's teacher? Mrs ....

3 How many children are in May's class? ....

4 What's the name of May's brother? ....

5 How old is May's brother? ....

Part 3
– 5 questions –

Listen and tick (✔) the box. There is one example.

Which is Sam's favourite sport?

1 Where's Kim?

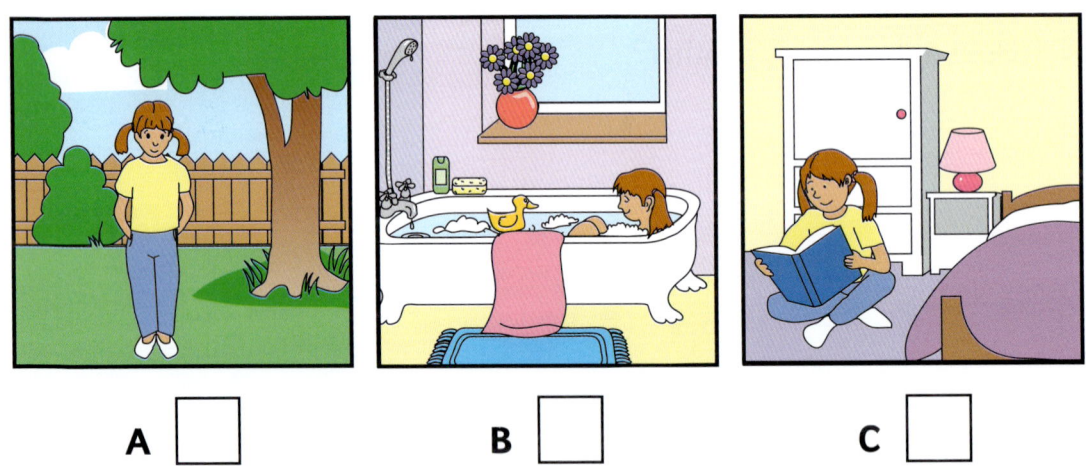

2 What's under Mum's hat?

Listening

3 What does May want for supper?

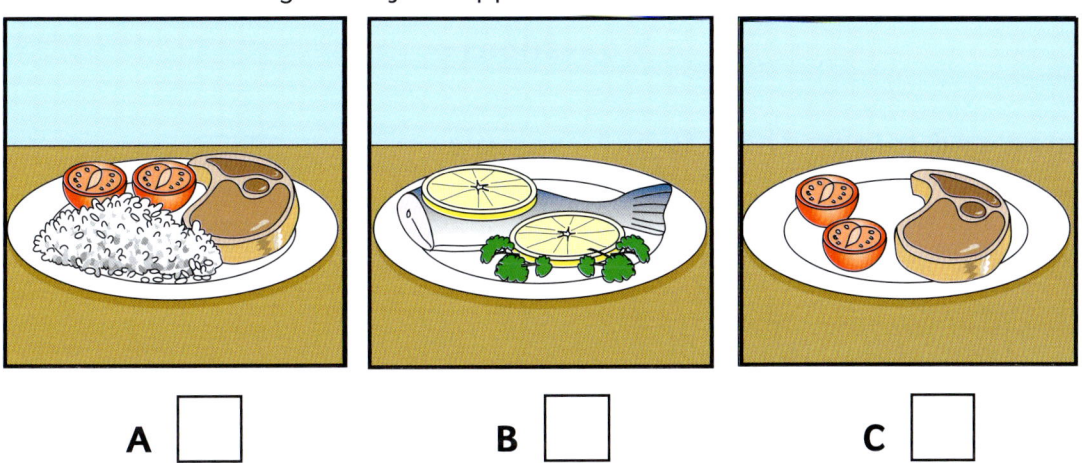

A ☐   B ☐   C ☐

4 Which woman is Sam's teacher?

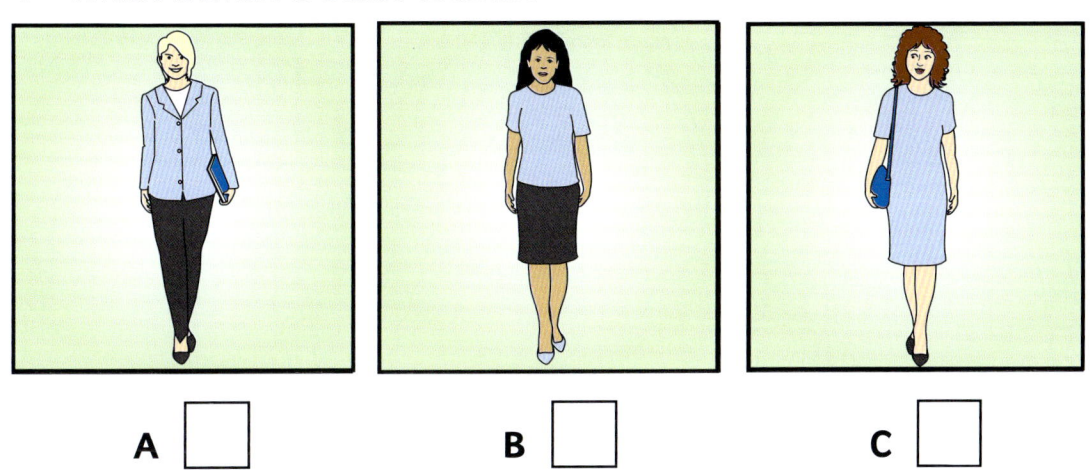

A ☐   B ☐   C ☐

5 What's Anna doing?

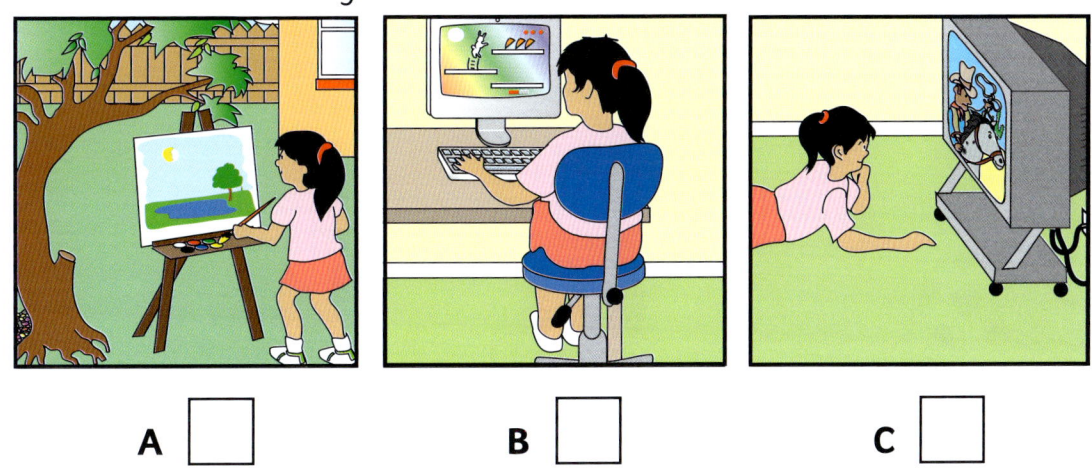

A ☐   B ☐   C ☐

Part 4
– 5 questions –

Listen and colour. There is one example.

Test 3
Reading and Writing

Part 1
– 5 questions –

Look and read. Put a tick (✓) or a cross (✗) in the box. There are two examples.

Examples

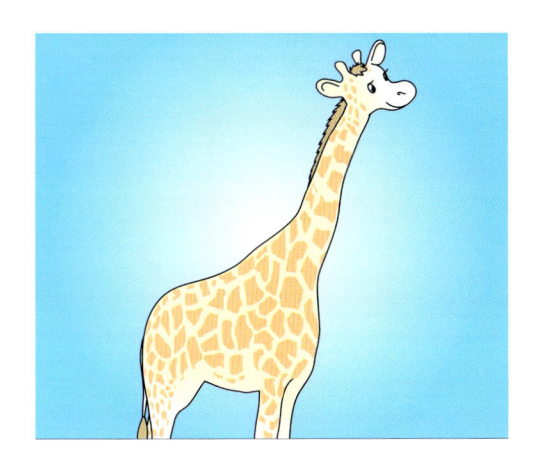

This is a giraffe. ✓

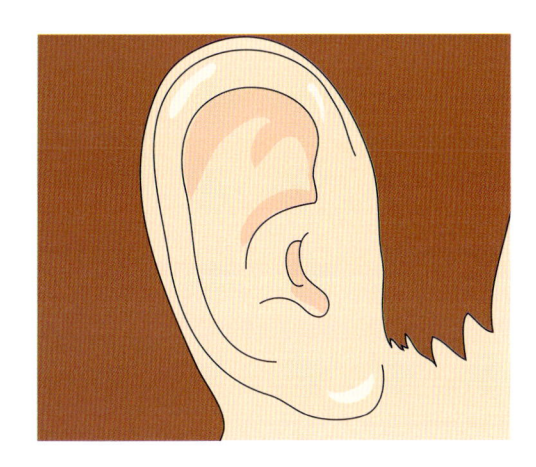

This is an eye. ✗

Questions

1   This is a foot. ☐

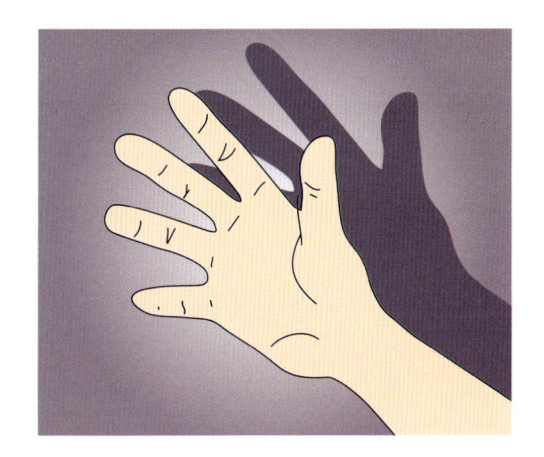

Test 3

2   This is a lime. ☐

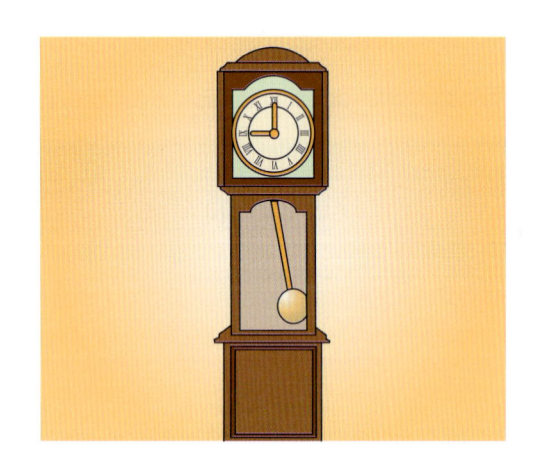

3   This is a watch. ☐

4   This is a tiger. ☐

5   This is a shell. ☐

40

Reading and Writing

Part 2
– 5 questions –

Look and read. Write yes or no.

Examples

A boy is playing with a robot. .... yes

There are four girls in the picture. .... no

Questions

1   The green monster is playing the guitar. ....

2   The woman is eating some birthday cake. ....

3   The man has got a camera. ....

4   A girl is singing a song. ....

5   There is a doll on the table. ....

Test 3

Part 3
– 5 questions –

Look at the pictures. Look at the letters. Write the words.

Example

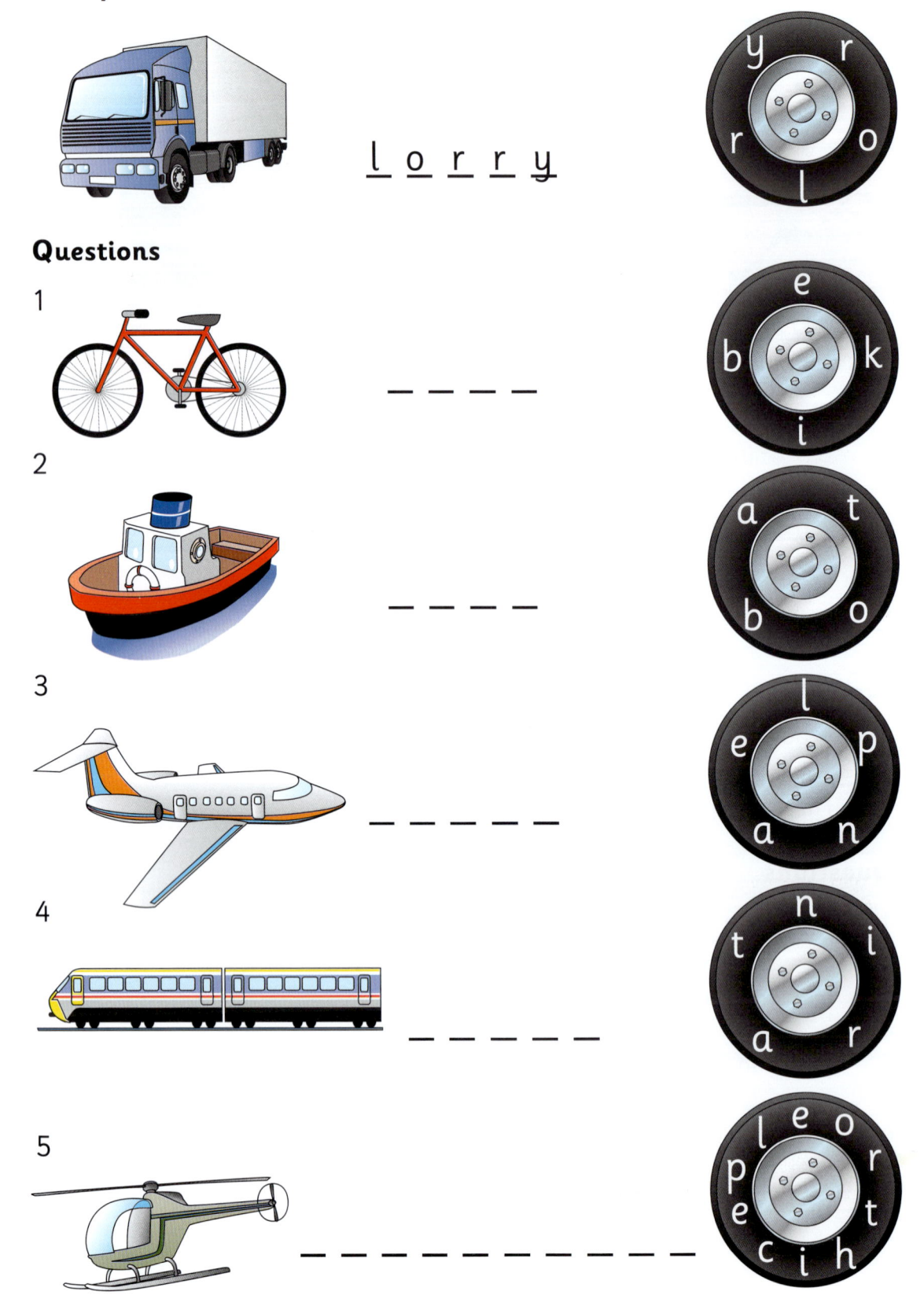

l o r r y

Questions

1 _ _ _ _

2 _ _ _ _

3 _ _ _ _ _

4 _ _ _ _ _

5 _ _ _ _ _ _ _ _ _

Reading and Writing

Part 4
– 5 questions –

Read this. Choose a word from the box. Write the correct word next to numbers 1–5. There is one example.

A classroom

I am in a school. A ....*teacher*.... gives lessons in me. She writes

on a big white **(1)** .... on my wall. Some

(2) .... learn in me. They sit on

(3) .... and there are desks in front of them. On the

desks, they have pencils and rulers. They read **(4)** .... ,

write stories, draw pictures, and play **(5)** .... in me.

What am I? I am a classroom.

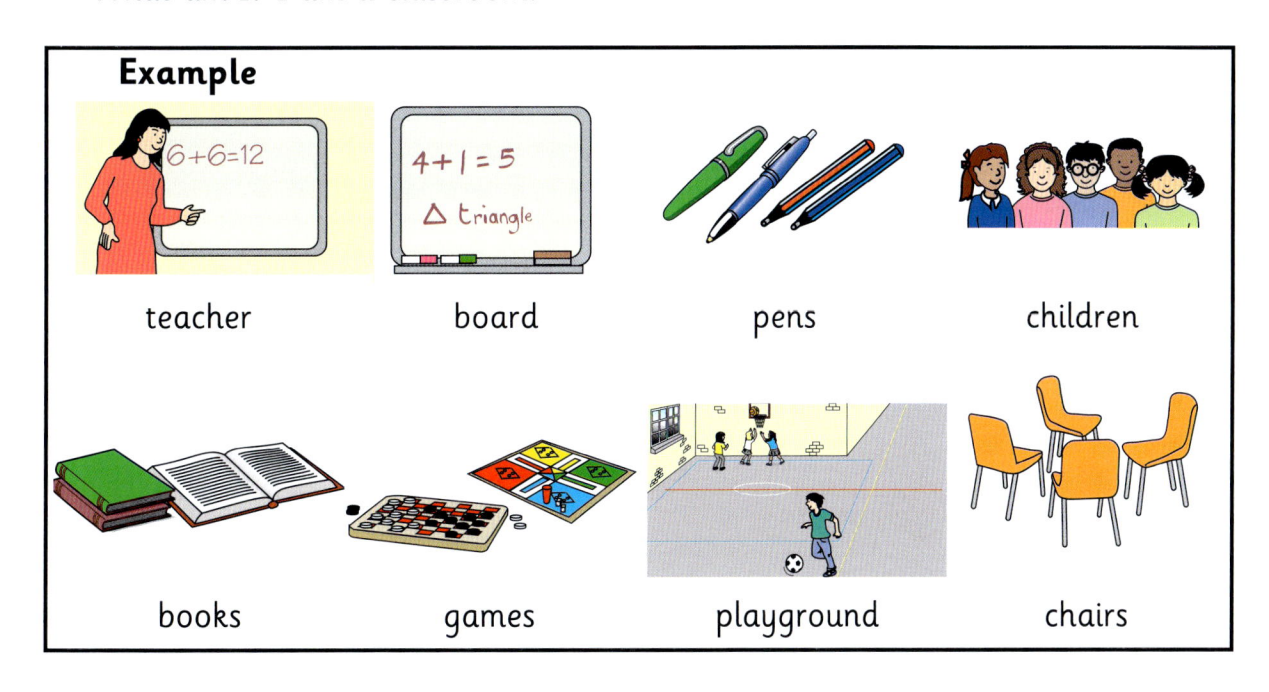

Example			
teacher	board	pens	children
books	games	playground	chairs

Test 3

Part 5
– 5 questions –

Look at the pictures and read the questions. Write one-word answers.

Examples

Where are the goats?   in the garden

What is the boy doing?   reading

Questions

1   What is the girl wearing?   a yellow ....

Reading and Writing

2   What is the black goat eating?   the ....

3   How many pears are there?   ....

4   Who is angry?   the ....

5   What is the boy doing now?   ....

Blank Page

Test 1
Speaking

SCENE CARD

47

Blank Page

OBJECT CARDS

Test 1 · Test 1 · Test 1 · Test 1 · Test 1 · Test 1 · Test 1 · Test 1

Blank Page

Test 2
Speaking

SCENE CARD

Blank Page

OBJECT CARDS

53

Blank Page

Blank Page

Test 3
Speaking

SCENE CARD

Blank Page

OBJECT CARDS

57